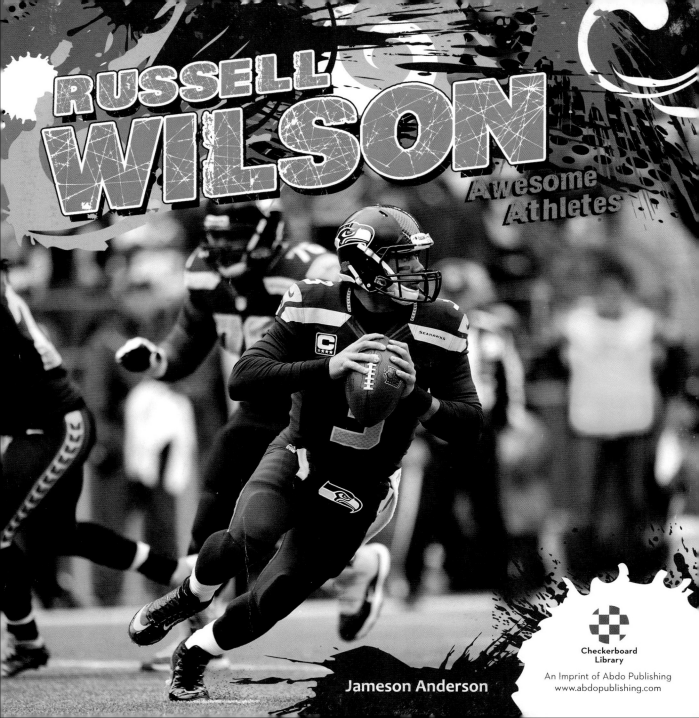

# RUSSELL WILSON

## Awesome Athletes

Jameson Anderson

Checkerboard Library

An Imprint of Abdo Publishing
www.abdopublishing.com

**www.abdopublishing.com**

Published by Abdo Publishing, a division of ABDO, PO Box 398166, Minneapolis, Minnesota 55439. Copyright © 2015 by Abdo Consulting Group, Inc. International copyrights reserved in all countries. No part of this book may be reproduced in any form without written permission from the publisher. Checkerboard Library™ is a trademark and logo of Abdo Publishing.

Printed in the United States of America, North Mankato, Minnesota.
052014
092014

THIS BOOK CONTAINS
RECYCLED MATERIALS

Cover Photo: AP Images
Interior Photos: AP Images pp. 1, 4, 5, 7, 9, 11, 13, 15, 17, 19, 21, 22, 25, 27, 29

Series Coordinator: Tamara L. Britton
Editors: Rochelle Baltzer, Megan M. Gunderson
Art Direction: Neil Klinepier

**Library of Congress Cataloging-in-Publication Data**

Anderson, Jameson.
  Russell Wilson / Jameson Anderson.
     pages cm. -- (Awesome athletes)
  Includes index.
  ISBN 978-1-62403-337-7
  1. Wilson, Russell, 1988---Juvenile literature. 2. Quarterbacks (Football)--United States--Biography--Juvenile literature. 3. Football players--United States--Biography--Juvenile literature. 4. Baseball players--United States--Biography--Juvenile literature. 5. Seattle Seahawks (Football team)--Juvenile literature. I. Title.
  GV939.WW545A64 2015
  796.332092--dc23
  [B]
                                  2014010903

# TABLE OF CONTENTS

# CHAMPIONS

**Super Bowl XLVIII featured the largest score spread in more than 20 years.**

On February 2, 2014, fans stood and cheered at MetLife Stadium in East Rutherford, New Jersey. Confetti was shot into the air above the players holding one of the most prized awards in all of sports, the Vince Lombardi Trophy. The Seattle Seahawks had just beaten the Denver Broncos 43–8 to win **Super Bowl** XLVIII.

Many fans were shocked at the score. Most experts had picked Denver to win. No one on the Seattle team had been to the Super Bowl before! But Seattle's quarterback, Russell Wilson, had led his offense with efficient play. He completed 18 of 25 of passes. He threw for 206 yards (188 m) and two touchdowns.

Russell Wilson with the Vince Lombardi Trophy. The prize is named after the famed Green Bay Packers coach who led his team to victory in Super Bowls I and II.

Some had thought Wilson was too short to play professional football. But he let the world know he was tall enough, quick enough, and smart enough to win. Wilson knew there was a great future ahead of him. He was just 25 years old, and it was only his second season in the **National Football League (NFL)**.

# HIGHLIGHT REEL

Russell Carrington Wilson was born in Cincinnati, Ohio.

## 1988

The Colorado Rockies drafted Wilson in the fourth round of the MLB Draft; he began playing in the minor leagues.

## 2010

On April 27, the Seattle Seahawks drafted Wilson with the 75th overall pick in the third round of the NFL Draft.

## 2012

## 2007

The Baltimore Orioles drafted Wilson in the 41st round of the MLB Draft; he declined to sign a contract.

## 2011

Wilson finished his college football career at the University of Wisconsin–Madison.

## 2014

Wilson and the Seattle Seahawks defeated the Denver Broncos in Super Bowl XLVIII.

# RUSSELL WILSON

**DOB:** November 29, 1988
**Ht:** 5'11"
**Wt:** 206
**Position:** QB
**Number:** 3

## CAREER STATISTICS:
Passing Yards: . . . . . . . . . . . . . . . . . 6,475
Passing Touchdowns: . . . . . . . . . . . . . 52
Rushing Yards: . . . . . . . . . . . . . . . . 1,028
Rushing Touchdowns: . . . . . . . . . . . . . . 5
Quarterback Rating: . . . . . . . . . . . . . 101.2

## AWARDS:
**Pepsi NFL Rookie of the Year:** 2012
**Pro Bowl:** 2012, 2013
**Senior Bowl:** 2011
**Super Bowl Champion:** 2014

# FAMILY, SPORTS & SCHOOL

Russell Carrington Wilson was born on November 29, 1988, in Cincinnati, Ohio.  His parents were Tammy and Harrison B. Wilson III.  His father was a lawyer and his mother worked as a legal nurse consultant.  Russell is their middle child.  He has an older brother, Harrison Wilson IV, and a younger sister, Anna.

Sports are a tradition in the Wilson family.  Russell's father played football and baseball at Dartmouth College.  And in 1980, his father was the last player cut from the San Diego Chargers preseason squad.

Russell's brother played baseball, football, and basketball in high school.  He continued with baseball and football in college.  Their sister is a basketball star who had college offers in eighth grade!

**Russell and his mother attended the White House Correspondents Association Annual Dinner in 2014.**

Education is also important in the Wilson family. Russell's grandfather, Harrison Wilson Jr., was president of Norfolk State University in Virginia. Before that, he was a football and basketball star at Kentucky State University. He recognized his grandson's athletic skills when Russell was very young.

Russell practiced football with his father and brother. Because they were both receivers, Russell chose to play quarterback. As a young boy, Russell learned to play baseball with a plastic ball and bat. Russell also played basketball with his brother. He never let Russell win! This just made Russell work harder.

Already, Russell was a three-sport kid. Later, he would have to make a difficult choice about which sport to pursue.

By the time Russell was ready for school, his family had moved to Virginia. He attended Collegiate School, a kindergarten through twelfth grade private school in Richmond. There, he became known for sports and academics.

Russell has admitted that he wasn't always the best-behaved student. He regrets that he would sometimes get in fights. As a teenager, his focus on his family's Christian religion taught him to be nicer and to respect people.

**At home, Russell got in trouble for throwing the football in the house! Yet at age nine, he was already impressing coaches with his arm. Today, Russell is seen as a great, accurate passer.**

**FUN FACT**

RUSSELL'S FATHER TAUGHT HIS KIDS THE IMPORTANCE OF BEING PRESENTABLE AND WELL-SPOKEN AFTER A GAME. RUSSELL EVEN PRACTICED SUPER BOWL SPEECHES!

# HIGH SCHOOL STAR

In 2004, in tenth grade, Russell's coach held an open competition for who would play quarterback. It was between Russell and another player who was a year older and taller. Russell won. But he would remember that moment. There would always be taller players who wanted to be quarterback.

Between seasons, Russell attended Manning Passing Academy. There, he learned quarterback skills from **NFL** great Peyton Manning.

Russell's junior season was a major success. The team went 11–0 and won the state championship. Russell also had good individual **statistics** in 2005. He threw for 3,287 yards (3,006 m) and 40 touchdowns. He had 634 rushing yards (580 m) for 15 touchdowns. He was named the Richmond Times-Dispatch Player of the Year.

Years after Russell attended Manning Passing Academy, the two met again in the NFL. In Super Bowl XLVIII, the Seahawks faced Manning's Denver Broncos!

Senior year, Russell threw for 3,009 yards (2,751 m). He scored 34 passing touchdowns. He rushed for 1,132 yards (1,035 m) and 18 touchdowns. Russell led the Collegiate Cougars to another state championship title.

In the state championship game, Russell was 21 for 37, passing for 291 yards (266 m) and two touchdowns. He rushed 30 times for another 223 yards (204 m) and three touchdowns. This earned him an appearance in *Sports Illustrated* magazine.

# CHOOSING COLLEGE

Football was Russell's favorite sport, but he worried he was too short to play in the **NFL**. Most NFL quarterbacks are at least 6 feet 2 inches tall (1 m 88 cm). Russell was just less than 5 feet 11 inches (1 m 80 cm). He jokingly asked his coach to say he was taller. He wanted **scouts** to notice him!

Russell also played baseball in high school. Senior year, he played shortstop and batted .467. This caught the attention of **Major League Baseball (MLB)** scouts. The Baltimore Orioles **drafted** him in June 2007.

Russell was picked in the forty-first round, as a second baseman. He was the 1,222nd overall pick. Russell was offered $1 million to sign a contract to play for the Orioles' **minor league** teams.

Russell had to make an important decision. He could take the money and play baseball. Or, he could go to college, play football, graduate, and try to get noticed by NFL scouts.

Russell's father convinced him to go to college. Many family members had gone to college and the Wilsons knew the value of education. So, Russell committed to play baseball and football for North Carolina State University (NC State) in Raleigh.

At NC State, Russell batted .296 his freshman year and .236 the following year. Junior year, he batted .306. He played shortstop and was a relief pitcher.

# NC STATE

At NC State, Russell focused on academics and two sports. He **redshirted** for football his freshman year. So every day, he woke up at four thirty in the morning and lifted weights with the football team. Then he went to class. In the afternoon, he played baseball.

In spring 2008, Russell played baseball and attended football practice. He was originally fifth on the quarterback depth chart. But by fall, he was starter in the opening game against South Carolina. He started 11 of 12 games in his first season with the Wolfpack.

Russell threw for two touchdowns in each of the final six games. He helped his team end the season with four straight wins.

Russell led the Atlantic Coast Conference (ACC) with 17 touchdown passes. He had just one **interception** in 275 attempts. After a knee injury in the PapaJohns.com Bowl against Rutgers on December 29, Russell's season was done.

Russell was named the first-team All-ACC quarterback. It was the first time a freshman quarterback had received the honor.

In his second season, Russell set an **NCAA** record with 379 pass attempts in a row without an **interception**. The streak spanned two seasons, ending on October 3, 2009, against Wake Forest. Russell had 3,287 yards (3,006 m) of total offense. He threw for 31 touchdowns, including 5 against Florida State to tie a school record.

# MINOR LEAGUES

On June 8, 2010, Russell was **drafted** into baseball a second time. This time, **MLB**'s Colorado Rockies took him with the 140th overall pick in the fourth round.

Russell played in the 2010 and 2011 seasons for **minor league** teams. He played second base for the Tri-City Dust Devils of Washington and the Asheville Tourists of North Carolina. In 93 games, he batted .229 and contributed 58 runs in 315 at-bats.

Meanwhile, Russell was team captain for the Wolfpack in 2010. He started all 13 games and completed 308 of 527 passes. He passed for 3,563 yards (3,258 m) and 28 touchdowns and rushed for another 9 touchdowns. He was showing the world that even a shorter quarterback could lead a team to victory.

Russell decided to participate in spring training for the Rockies in 2011. His coaches at NC State said that he needed to either focus on baseball or football.

Russell chose to focus on football.

Russell knew that playing for a bigger school could get him more attention from **NFL scouts**. So, he transferred to the University of Wisconsin–Madison to play. Honoring his promise to his dad, Russell graduated from NC State with a degree in broadcasting and communications. At Wisconsin, he would enroll in a graduate program.

Asheville Tourists, 2011

## LOSING HIS FATHER

RUSSELL'S FATHER SUFFERED FROM DIABETES. HE LOST A LEG AS WELL AS HIS EYESIGHT TO THE DISEASE. SO, RUSSELL'S BROTHER WOULD NARRATE NC STATE GAMES FOR HIM. ON JUNE 9, 2010, RUSSELL'S FATHER DIED. RUSSELL WAS GLAD HIS FATHER LIVED TO SEE HIM GET DRAFTED.

# GO BADGERS!

Russell was determined to make it as a quarterback for the University of Wisconsin Badgers. He drove 17 hours straight from Richmond to Madison just to pick up a copy of the team's playbook. He memorized it over the Fourth of July weekend. Russell wanted to be ready to make a good impression on his coaches.

A transfer to Wisconsin put Russell on a bigger stage. He was now playing in the Big Ten Conference. Doing well meant a better chance at the **NFL**. Russell came in as a starter and never looked back.

Russell's first game starting as a Badger was against the University of Las Vegas on September 1, 2011. Russell completed 10 of 13 passes for 255 yards (233 m) and two touchdowns. This impressive start earned Russell Big Ten Offensive Player of the Week.

Two weeks later, Madison faced Northern Illinois. Russell pulled out a season-best 23 of 32 passes for 347

**FUN FACT**

RUSSELL WAS ONE OF FOUR PLAYERS TO TALLY MORE THAN 1,000 RUSHING YARDS (914 M) AND MORE THAN 5,000 PASSING YARDS (4,572 M) IN HIS COLLEGE CAREER.

yards (317 m). The next week, he threw for 345 yards (315 m) against South Dakota. With that, he became the team's first player to throw for at least 325 yards twice in the same season.

**Wisconsin defeated the University of Las Vegas 51–17 on September 1, 2011.**

Russell wore No. 16 for Wisconsin and NC State.

Under Russell's leadership, the Badgers started the 2011 season 6–0. They finished with an 11–3 record. This took them to the Big Ten Championship game against Michigan State on December 3.

Russell went 17 for 24, passing for 187 yards (171 m) and three touchdowns with no **interceptions**. This was Russell's thirty-seventh game in a row throwing a touchdown pass, which broke the **NCAA** record. Wisconsin won the game 42–39. Russell was named the Grange-Griffin Big Ten Championship Game Most Valuable Player (MVP).

That win took Wisconsin to the Rose Bowl. They faced Oregon on January 2, 2012. Russell was responsible for three touchdowns, but the Badgers lost 45–38.

In just one season at Wisconsin, Russell left his name in the record books. He was first in the Big Ten with 3,513 total yards (3,212 m) and 39 touchdowns. He broke Wisconsin's single-season record for passing yards with 3,175 (2,903 m). He also broke school records with 33 touchdown passes and 225 completions.

Russell finished ninth in the running for the **Heisman Trophy**. He threw for the most yards per pass in the Big Ten with an average of 10.3 yards (9.4 m) per pass. That **stat** made him second in the NCAA after Baylor's Robert Griffin III. Griffin would go on to be starting quarterback for the Washington Redskins. He and Russell were **drafted** the same year.

# NFL DRAFT

The 2011 season was a success for Wilson. He was named the Grese-Brees Big Ten Quarterback of the year. He was invited to play in the Senior Bowl and participate in the **NFL** combine.

Most **scouts** told Wilson that he would be **drafted** during the 2012 NFL Draft. But experts had a hard time predicting exactly when Wilson would be taken. Other taller quarterbacks were in the draft that year. Despite Wilson's achievements, people worried about his ability to see over the **line of scrimmage**.

Few expected Wilson to be drafted by the Seattle Seahawks. They had just acquired Green Bay Packers quarterback Matt Flynn. Most Seattle fans expected Flynn to be the team's quarterback of the future.

Wilson had a strong preseason with the Seahawks. He made his debut against the Arizona Cardinals on September 9, 2012, in a 20–16 loss.

The Seahawks **drafted** Wilson in the third round of the **NFL** Draft on April 27, 2012. He was the seventy-fifth overall pick and the sixth quarterback selected. Wilson signed a four-year, $2.99 million contract on May 7. He would put on the No. 3 jersey for the Seahawks.

# ROOKIE SEASON

In August 2012, Seahawks coaches officially named Wilson the team's starting quarterback. In just his second game, his 75 percent completion rating broke a team record. He completed 15 of 20 passes for 151 yards (138 m). The Seahawks beat the Dallas Cowboys 27–7.

The Seahawks finished the season 11–5, which sent them to the **playoffs**. They defeated the Washington Redskins 24–14 in the Wild Card game. Then they lost the NFC Divisional game to the Atlanta Falcons 30–28. Wilson passed for 385 yards (352 m) and two touchdowns. He rushed for another 60 yards (55 m) and one touchdown.

Wilson finished the regular season with a Seahawks record 100.0 passer rating. He also tied Peyton Manning for most touchdown passes by a **rookie** with 26. Wilson's second **NFL** season was even more successful. Yet near its end, **MLB** came knocking again. The Texas

Rangers selected Wilson in the Rule 5 **Draft** on December 13, 2013. Teams are able to draft players who have already been drafted but aren't on major league teams.

Wilson of course wasn't going to give up his job as quarterback of the Seahawks. But, he did visit with the Rangers to help draw attention to the baseball program. Wilson may never leave football to play baseball, but if he does, the Rangers have rights to him.

**Wilson in his record-breaking game against Dallas on September 16, 2012.**

# LOOKING AHEAD

Wilson's second pro season led him to the ultimate stage, the **Super Bowl**. Everything he had dreamed of as a young boy playing football had come true. It also was the team's first-ever Super Bowl title.

To get there, Wilson led his team to a 13–3 regular-season record. The Seahawks defeated the New Orleans Saints 23–15 to win the division. They took down the San Francisco 49ers to win the conference 23–17. Wilson completed 16 of 25 passes for 215 yards (197 m) and a touchdown to help the Seahawks reach the big game.

Off the field, Wilson's success has led to **endorsement** deals with Nike, Alaska Airlines, EA Sports, Levi's, and other companies. Wilson also maintains a focus on charity work. He donates money for every touchdown. He also organizes the Russell Wilson Passing Academy camp for kids, which supports **diabetes** research.

**FUN FACT** WHEN WILSON WON THE SUPER BOWL, HE WAS STILL ON HIS ROOKIE CONTRACT. HIS SALARY IN 2013 WAS JUST OVER $526,000. THAT'S LESS THAN PEYTON MANNING MADE IN A SINGLE GAME!

For a young quarterback with a **Super Bowl** win already in his trophy case, Russell Wilson is off to a great start. Wilson showed the world that height isn't the only measure of a quarterback. He could now be seen as one of the game's future greats.

In 16 starts his second season, Wilson again had 26 passing touchdowns. He had 3,357 total passing yards (3,070 m) and 539 (493 m) rushing for another 4 touchdowns.

# GLOSSARY

**diabetes** - a disease in which the body cannot properly absorb normal amounts of sugar and starch.

**draft** - an event during which sports teams choose new players. Choosing new players is known as drafting them.

**endorsement** - the act of publicly recommending a product or service in exchange for money.

**Heisman Trophy** - an award given each year to the most outstanding player in college football.

**interception** - a pass thrown by a quarterback that is caught by a player on the opposing team.

**line of scrimmage** - a line across a football field based on the ball's location at the end of a play. Players may not cross the line until the next play begins.

**Major League Baseball (MLB)** - the highest level of professional baseball. It is made up of the American League (AL) and the National League (NL).

**minor leagues** - the five classes of professional baseball that are lower level than the major leagues.

**National Football League (NFL)** - the highest level of professional football. It is made up of the American Football Conference (AFC) and the National Football Conference (NFC).

**NCAA** - National Collegiate Athletic Association.  The NCAA supports student athletes on and off the field.  It creates the rules for fair and safe play.

**playoffs** - a series of games that determine which team will win a championship.

**redshirt** - to limit a college athlete's participation in a sport for one school year.

**rookie** - a first-year player in a professional sport.

**scout** - a person who evaluates the talent of amateur athletes to determine if they would have success in the pros.

**statistics** - also called stats.  Numbers that represent pieces of information about a game or player.  Passing yards, touchdowns, and tackles are a few football statistics.

**Super Bowl** - the annual National Football League (NFL) championship game.  It is played by the winners of the American and National Conferences.

# WEBSITES

To learn more about Awesome Athletes, visit **booklinks.abdopublishing.com**.  These links are routinely monitored and updated to provide the most current information available.

# INDEX